Finding God

Finding God

JAMES JONES

Darton, Longman and Todd
London

First published in 1987 by
Darton, Longman and Todd Ltd
89 Lillie Road, London SW6 1UD

© 1987 James Jones

ISBN 0 232 51710 X

British Library Cataloguing in Publication Data

Jones, James, *1948–*
  Finding God.
  1. God
  I. Title
  231   BT102

  ISBN 0–232–51710–X

Phototypeset by
Input Typesetting Ltd, London SW19 8DR
Printed and bound in Great Britain by
Anchor Brendon Ltd
Tiptree, Essex

To Sarah

Contents

Acknowledgements

Gill Snow, Catriona Boughton and Anne Stanford have each played a part in preparing this book for publication. I thank them most warmly.

I owe a debt of gratitude to Canon Paul Berg, my colleague, for his encouragement and for his detailed comments and suggestions. I have benefited too from the kindness of Grace who provided the haven in which to write.

I thank also the staff, Church leaders and the family of Christ Church, Clifton, where my wife Sarah and I and our children have known the love of God.

Finally I would like to acknowledge and thank all those fellow seekers after God whose questions and observations have given this book its shape.

J.J.
1986

1

A Pattern

I was walking along the beach at Exmouth. It was in the early hours of the morning. A gang of us had driven down there after a night out. It was a time of budding romances and for some even youthful marriages. While several couples ran along the sands I stood there alone gazing at the stars. The air was fresh with the smell of the sea, the silence made louder by the sound of distant waves. The occasional shouts and laughter of courting couples now far along the beach echoed around and made me aware of my aloneness. I was not lonely. I was simply aware that I stood alone.

I felt something which I thought at the time to be very unusual. I wanted somehow to embrace the vast creation which spanned above and around me. The spacious galaxy of stars, the ocean that lay beyond the ebbing tide, the stretch of sand that bordered the elements of earth and water. I wanted to reach out and hold creation to me. I wanted to make it all a part of me. It seems strange to write all this. But I wanted to feed upon it; to eat it; to be united with it. I wanted it to be in me and me in it. I was not then, neither am I now, given to mystical experiences. But my imagination was taking me to realms I had never been to before.

It was in those moments however that I wondered again whether or not anything really lay beyond this creation. Was it fanciful or reasonable to believe in God? And what sort of God anyway was I imagining? Was it something or someone?

As I walked along the beach towards the sea it no longer felt a flight of fancy to believe that what I saw around me had actually been created. It bore the hallmark of design.

I knew that the arguments for and against the existence of God were evenly matched. Neither was conclusive. But here on the beach, instinctively, I found the argument of design persuasive. I knew it could not prove the existence of God and yet it offered an insight into the possibility of God.

A few years later I heard the story of a famous and devout scientist who owned a model of the universe which stood on his study desk. It was a precise and beautiful model of the planets circling the sun. A colleague, a renowned atheist, noticed the model and enquired who had made it. The scientist seized his opportunity and, with a pretence of seriousness, informed his friend that nobody had made the thing and that it had appeared out of nowhere. The atheist was understandably unimpressed and grew impatient. 'Don't be ridiculous. Just tell me who made it.' But the scientist pressed his point with force and humour. 'My dear friend, if you find it so difficult to believe that this simple model exists without a creator, how foolish of you to believe that the real thing, a billion times greater, could exist without a creator.'

This is not of course proof. It is a signpost along the way. It is an indicator in the experiment of finding God. Certainly on that Devon beach I sensed that I was moving forward. And it appears from all the surveys that I was in step with the vast majority who believe in some force at work in the universe. I stood by the water's edge. The tide had begun to turn. The design suggests a designer.

I looked at my watch. I had never been to Japan, neither had I seen the oriental men and women who make watches nor even those who make the robots that now make the watches, yet I confidently believed that the Japanese wristwatch which told me that it was now 3.30 on Saturday morning had been made by somebody. Its intricate design and inner workings, which by comparison with the human brain were naive, suggested convincingly that it possessed a maker. I believed it. It did not seem such a rash and irrational belief. Neither did the belief in the possibility of a creative force.

As I walked back to the car and rejoined my friends I tried to say something about what I was feeling. The words were clumsy. They obviously did not fit the mood of the moment. 'Isn't it wonderful to believe that there might be a God beyond all this?' The words seemed out of place and out of step with the others. But to wonder at and meditate on the design of the universe was for me an important step forward.

Take some obviously manufactured article and consider its design. A watch . . . a pen . . . a chair . . . a book. Imagine the business of designing and manufacturing it. Then consider a work of art. A painting . . . a vase . . . some pottery . . . a sculpture.

Try to picture the person at work creating what you see before you.

Fix your mind on some object of the natural world. A tree . . . a flower . . . an animal. Consider its pattern. Meditate on its design. Imagine the possibility of a designer. And say this prayer:

> *'God, you may be there after all. The designer of the world and of me.'*

And then be still.

2

A Force

When we discovered that my wife was pregnant I was filled with dread. Gone were the days when the husband waited outside the maternity suite to be summoned with the news of the arrival of a son or a daughter. Social pressures make it almost mandatory for the husband not only to be present but to assist actively in the delivery of the child. To describe my attitude to things medical as squeamish would be an understatement. The smell of a hospital causes the walls to spin round. The sight of a drop of blood has me reeling. So I viewed the prospect of attending the birth of our first child with mixed feelings. Looking back I am now grateful for the social pressures (and for the encouragement of my wife) that forced me to be present. Having been with Sarah for the birth of both our children there is nothing in the world that would ever keep me away. On the first occasion I was so caught up with the joy of the moment that, when the doctor asked me to assist in directing the light while she sewed some stitches, I came to her aid like an experienced midwife. It was only afterwards when I got home and was on the telephone recounting my brave contribution to the wonderful event that the walls began to move.

What is it about the birth of children that inspires our wonder? Why do women allow themselves to go through with it more than once? I could not understand how my wife, within weeks of having one, could be talking of having another. 'Don't you remember what it's like?'

Holding your own child for the first time is a beautiful and profoundly personal moment. You, the parent, are embracing this child who was once a part of you and is now separate from you. As persons you are separate yet bound together. This child belongs to you and you belong to the child. And here begins a relationship that is personal and intimate. But where did we get this ability to relate to each other in this personal way?

Many people believe in a creative force. They would talk of God as some thing rather than some person. They reject the idea of a personal God as childish. Obviously there are many immature views of the world that ought to be discarded by the adult mind, not least the one which imagines God resplendent with white beard enthroned in the clouds. But it is worth considering that whatever made us persons, to have and enjoy personal relationships such as that between a parent and child, presumably possesses the same ability, for where else did we get it from? Surely the creator cannot be less than the creature. It is difficult to imagine that a force, some impersonal or subpersonal thing, could be the author of persons. In a sentence, it is hard to believe (though admittedly not impossible) that PERSONS were made by a THING, something less than themselves, and so is it unreasonable to believe that whatever created human beings is at least a personal

6

force able to vest in them the capacity for personal relationships?

The force may of course be more than personal, but surely not less. So when we begin to imagine what sort of force is at work in the universe, it is perhaps not so childish to begin to talk about 'he' or even 'she' rather than 'it'.

Think about a relationship which you greatly value. With a friend. Your marriage. In the family. With a colleague. Explore the reasons why this relationship means so much to you.

Accepting that the ability to enjoy and be fulfilled in this relationship may come ultimately from God, make this prayer:

> *'If you are the creator of people, I thank you, God, for creating me.'*

Then be still again.

3

Escapism

The lower examination hall at university was an awesome place. A large subterranean vault artificially lit where desks were set out in serried ranks. I vividly remember filing in with several hundred other students one Monday morning in May for the start of my final examinations. The papers were face down on the desk and I peered through the thin paper to try to decipher what questions were printed on the other side, in the hope of gaining some small advantage. My mouth went dry and my heart beat a little faster. The atmosphere was strained all the more by anxious coughing and the padding of the invigilators' Hush Puppies as they crept around the hall checking that everybody had the right papers. All eyes were fixed on the clock. Its hands were moving steadily towards nine o'clock. Our hands began nervously to finger the paper. All were poised for the chief invigilator to tell us to begin, when suddenly the atmosphere was shattered by a piercing and hysterical scream from a girl in the front row. 'Get me out of here. . .! I can't stand it any more . . .' The invigilators rushed to the poor girl, who was screaming and moaning, and taking her by the arms and legs carried her out as quickly as possible and without much dignity. Blood drained from the face of every student. Dry mouths were now parched. Hearts that had beat a little faster were now racing. I felt sick. The screams and moans faded in the distant corridor. 'You may now begin . . .' The papers turned rather slowly.

The previous day being Sunday, and in particular the Sunday before finals, had seen a strange phenomenon. It happened every year. Attendance at morning service in the university chapel soared to a capacity congregation. People who had been nowhere near a church in the previous year were to be found literally queuing for a pew. I imagine that many were praying the same simple prayer, direct and to the point: 'O God, help me pass my exams.' Cynical observers of this annual pilgrimage added another festival to the church's calendar: 'Insurance Sunday'.

It is not surprising that such behaviour results in religion being dismissed as escapism. There are many situations in which human beings who have felt out of their depth have turned to God. War, death, divorce, unemployment, illness, are often times when we look beyond ourselves for some help and comfort. And to turn to God is without doubt a form of escapism. But that does not mean that God is not there and that religion is untrue. Attempting to escape may be a very sensible thing to do. Anyone who has been chased by a bull would agree. Escapism is a comment on the truth about man rather than about God. A child often escapes to his parents when he finds himself in some sort of trouble. Such behaviour tells us something about children and their needs. It does not disprove the existence of the parents.

It is at the very time when people begin to feel a need for God that they are often overwhelmed with doubt. In my own search I came to realise that, for various reasons, some clear and some not, I needed to find God. And it began to worry me that I might be making it all up, convincing myself, satisfying my own need of intellectual and emotional security. I began to ask myself, 'Is faith a psychological "con trick"? Am I deluding myself?' The issue came to a head for me when one day a friend dismissed my search for God with the line, 'Of course, your problem is that you *need* to believe in God.' I became very defensive and denied such a suggestion fiercely. When I later reflected on the argument I came to realise that I *did* need to believe in God. But I also came to see that to say that I needed God said nothing at all about whether or not God existed. I was being trapped in the cul-de-sac which implies that, because a person needs God, therefore God does not exist. But such a line of argument is as illogical as saying that my wife does not exist but is merely the product of my need to love and be loved. So I came to realise that there was no shame in admitting my own needs, nor was there any weakening of the intellectual case for God by acknowledging that much, though not all, religious behaviour is in a sense escapist.

We all have different reasons for escaping to God for each of us has different needs. It is an important part of the search to be aware as much as possible of what those needs exactly are. These are some of the common needs that many of us have.

There is an intellectual need – I need to find satis-

factory answers as to the origin and destiny of the universe.

There is a spiritual need – I need to discover some greater purpose for my own existence.

There is an emotional need – I need to feel the presence and help of some greater power.

As you explore these needs be honest with yourself. There is no shame in acknowledging need, although there may be a denting of your pride. Writing down your thoughts could be helpful.

Then turn these thoughts into a prayer:

'God, this is me. These are my needs.'

Jesus said: 'Come to me, all you who labour and are overburdened, and I will give you rest . . . learn from me.' (Matt. 11:28)

4

Adventure

We could not believe our luck. My wife and I, against our better judgment, had started to follow the progress of a glorified game of bingo in our daily newspaper. Our Saturday edition told us that we now possessed all the numbers to claim the week's prize, which stood at £80,000. We double-checked all the numbers again just to make sure there was no mistake. We could hardly contain our excitement as I dialled the newspaper to stake our claim. £80,000! We talked about how we would spend it and had it all planned within a few minutes. The newspaper's number was engaged. We tried all morning. I rang the operator. 'No, they haven't left the phone off the hook. I suggest you listen to the news.' The lunch-time bulletin informed us that there were long queues outside a certain newspaper office and that the switchboard was jammed with tens of thousands of callers, all claiming their £80,000 prize. Oh, well, a ridiculous game anyway!

Nevertheless it gave us a moment to daydream about what we would do with such wealth. A new car, some new clothes, a good holiday, a few gifts to friends in need, and the rest to be saved for a rainy day. Just the planning was an adventure. Like many, we were trapped in an unadventurous rut and dreamt of money as a means of breaking out of the prison in search of adventure. For many of us to be rich means to be free. To be rich means to be able to choose what you want to do and to be. To be rich gives us the power to shape our own destiny and to taste adventure.

When adventure is lacking we can turn to soap operas and novels. They provide us with heroes and heroines through whom we can live out a life of high adventure. Frederick Forsyth, Catherine Cookson and Jeffrey Archer give us a passport to adventure. We lose ourselves in the dramatic exploits of their heroes and find fulfilment in their adventures. *Dallas* and *Dynasty* have glued millions to their television sets. We have sat on the edge of our seats dismissing them as rubbish, while reaching for the box of tissues and making sure we are in for the next episode. We crave for adventure, and when we are denied it we feel something is missing.

Some years ago when I was a regular commuter to London I came across some graffiti which, in letters a metre high, stretched for a hundred metres along a wall that ran parallel with the railway line. 'The same thing every day tube – work – tube – TV – armchair – sleep – tube – work – tube – how much more can you take – one in five cracks up – one in ten goes mad.'

The daily routine had stifled any sense of adventure for the graffito artist.

Men and women, both out of work and in work, are frustrated when the experience of adventure is withheld. It is part of our nature to have goals and ambitions and to work to achieve and conquer them. The spirit of adventure is in our souls, put there by the one who made us. The goals and ambitions that we strive after can be tainted with evil, and the means of achieving and succeeding can become corrupt. But the quest for adventure is an essential part of human nature. And it is there because the spirit of adventure is first and foremost to be found in the nature of God who made us.

For those of us drawn to men and women of adventure, Jesus has a powerful attraction. In him we glimpse this free and adventurous spirit: undaunted by obstacles, unpredictable, uninhibited by opposition, energetic, imaginative, persuasive, compassionate, sensitive, disturbing, controversial. A reading of the gospel inspires an endless flow of adjectives. Here is adventure personified. And one of the attractions of Jesus to the men and women of his day was this spirit of adventure. To those that would follow he offered adventure. He gave them the opportunity to break out of their prisons and to begin to shape their own destiny. The adventure led them to undreamed-of heights and unimaginable depths. But the adventure, for all its risks and uncertainties, appealed to some deep-seated instinct.

The attraction of this man is no less strong some two thousand years later as we ourselves dream of adventure.

Think of a film, TV programme or book that has made an impact on you. And dwell on those aspects of the story that gripped you. Which characters did you feel most for? What episode did you find most absorbing? Did the story end in the way you wanted? How would you have changed it? What do you feel these thoughts say to you about yourself?

Turn this exploration into a prayer:

'God, I dream of adventure. I believe this thirst for adventure comes from you.'

Find some time to read the gospel of Mark.

Jesus said: 'I have come so that they may have life and have it to the full.' (John 10:10)

5

Fulfilment

One of the disappointments of no longer being a child was that Christmases never again had quite the same magical excitement. As I grew older they were still great fun. But something was missing. And I remember distinctly as a young teenager hankering after, and even trying to recreate within me, those childish longings and fulfilments. But they were gone. The sheer thrill of a child waiting uncertainly and then possessing a coveted present was now the object of adolescent nostalgia. Of course the fulfilment that came from acquiring those longed-for presents was always short-lived. Either the novelty wore off or the present fell victim to the designs of a younger brother and lay in ruins. In the event this toy, which came with promises of blissful happiness, was now discarded and gave way to ideas of other acquisitions, such as a birthday present, just a bit bigger and better, which needless to say would make me really happy. And so it went on.

I came to discover that, although there was something unique about a child's excitement, this desire to find fulfilment and happiness in acquiring new possessions was in everybody. The stereo system given to me on my twenty-first birthday, the first car, the presents at our wedding, are just some of the good things that brought a lot of happiness. But, like the childhood presents, the novelty of all these things soon wore off and they were being taken for granted. Even now my wife and I have a list of some of the things we want to get when we have the money. The compiling of the list and the prospect of buying the much-needed car-seats for the children and some winter clothes for the family give a sense of an inner something-or-other. When we get them we shall be pleased, genuinely pleased, but soon they will become commonplace. The fulfilment derived from these acquisitions is linked to our thirst for adventure. Creation is both spiritual and material. And the material things certainly add to our enjoyment. There will of course be moral issues about the worldwide imbalance of material riches, but to reject the material in favour of the spiritual would be to deny that God created them both.

These good things which I believe come from God can, however, be misleading if we think that in them alone we will find the secret of life's happiness. The fulfilment these things bring is often intense, but very fleeting. It is like quenching our thirst with salt water. The first satisfying gulp leaves you craving for more. Whether the object of our desire is a car or a child's bicycle, a doll's house or the real thing, the thirst for fulfilment is never fully satisfied by these waters. They leave us thirsty for something else.

Think about some possession which brought excitement to your life. Thank God for the happiness it gave you.

17

'God, I thank you for the enjoyment of acquiring new things. Show me what it is that brings lasting happiness and true fulfilment.'

Jesus said: 'I have told you this so that my own joy may be in you and your joy be complete.' (John 15:11)

6

Purpose

One of my dreams is to go on a luxury cruise in the sun.

I dream of a rich benefactor inviting us to join him for a holiday on his luxury cruiser. He will pay for everything. All we have to do is to arrive with our suitcases at the quayside in time for the sailing.

The ship sets sail and within a few days we are in the sun. Everything you can imagine is on board. The food is superb and the entertainment allows you to indulge all your desires. There are swimming pools, saunas and comfortable beds. Your host welcomes you and invites you to eat, drink and be merry. And you have no problm in wholeheartedly accepting this invitation. This is the stuff dreams are made on! Imagine, however, if the cruise were to develop along the following lines.

After two weeks sailing around in the sun the novelty is beginning to wear off, only slightly, and you wonder how much longer the cruise will last and what your destination might be. However you do not wish to appear ungrateful so you stifle the questions in the company of your host.

After six weeks cruising the dream has begun to resemble something of an endurance test. You have had a surfeit of good food, you wonder whether your heart could stand another sauna, and frankly you have become rather bored with sunbathing for hours each day. But nobody else seems to be bothered – at least on the surface – so you suppress the questions and carry on eating, drinking and being as merry as possible in the circumstances.

After ten years the dream has become a nightmare. You can contain yourself no longer and grab your host by the lapels. 'Look, tell me, where are we going? What's this all about? I can't take any more of it! When is this cruise going to finish?'

The scenario is far-fetched. But not too ridiculous. For we exist on this planet in a similar way. Earth, rather like a ship, cruises through space. Most of the time we are caught up in the business of making ends meet so that we can eat, drink and be comfortable. But every so often the travellers begin to wonder what it is all about. Where are we going? What is our destination? Are we on some glorified mystery tour where everything is a secret or is there some purpose to the journey that is for all of us to know? Many of us suppress the questions, either because nobody else we know seems to be concerned with them or because the little we do know is more comfortable than that of which we are ignorant. But, rather like the air bubbles in a stretch of badly hung wallpaper, which will not go away and when you press them emerge in another place, so too the questions will not disappear. Relentlessly they keep popping up in our minds and disturb our hearts.

A novelist from France put the question like this:

> Get up, tramway, four hours
> at the office or in the factory,

a meal, tramway, four hours work,
a meal, sleep and
Monday
Tuesday
Wednesday
Thursday
Friday
Saturday
in the same rhythm
one follows this path
without difficulty
most of the time.
One day however
arises the question
Why?

(A. Camus, 'The Myth of Sisyphus')

Basically what we are all looking for at some stage or other in our life is a purpose for our existence. This quest is in the heart of every single person.

This is how we live from day to day. We set ourselves goals and make plans accordingly. The person at work has targets to achieve which he either sets for himself or has handed down from above. The parent in the home has a routine which is based on getting things done so that the family can be cared for. The daily routine has a purpose.

In fact if men and women are denied a purpose to their daily life they quickly become demoralised. This is the curse of unemployment. Anyone who has been unemployed will know the feeling of waking up to yet another day of boredom and rejection; not having anything to do day after day in the end makes you lethargic, saps all your energy, and renders you almost incapable of doing a job in the future. When a man or woman no longer sees any purpose in everyday living he or she becomes depressed. It is as if human beings were made with a fundamental need to find a purpose for their existence.

Just as we need to find some purpose for our lives on a day-to-day basis, so we also need to find some purpose for the whole of our lives, so that, even though we may be engaged in work that is thoroughly absorbing and provides us with short-term goals, we are still left wondering about and hankering after some overall purpose. We need to know why we are here and what we should be doing with our lives. We need to know what it is all leading up to.

It is to this quest for purpose that Jesus speaks directly. To put it simply, he says we are on a journey which begins and ends with God.

Spend some time exploring what your goals are. What is the purpose of your work, be it paid or unpaid, be it outside or inside the home?

'God, I feel the need to find some overall purpose. Show me the purpose of my life.'

'Thomas said, ". . . how can we know the way?" Jesus said: "I am the Way".' (John 14:5–6)

7

Forgiveness

In common with many others, there are things in my
life of which I am deeply ashamed. Some are too
personal and hurtful for me to admit to anyone. The
following example is from my youth, but the thought
of it still fills me with a profound disappointment
and reminds me of my true nature. I had got into a
fight with another boy who happened to be an
orphan. In order to get my own back on him I said
that I was glad that his parents were dead. Even as
I recall these words I feel their shame. In the hubbub
of this schoolboy fight I am not sure to this day
whether he heard them. Yet the sense of shame was
there. Even though the boy was older and a bully it
did not detract from the appalling evil of expressing
satisfaction at the death of his parents. How could
I have said such a thing? My conscience was seared.
How I longed that the words could be unsaid, the
feelings unfelt and the deed undone. Even at that
relatively early age there was an awareness that all
was not right within and a longing that the
conscience could somehow be cleared. There may
have been some hope had the pain of this experience
prevented me from ever again behaving in such a
destructive manner. Sadly, although as the years
passed I became more adult and more sophisticated

in my dealings with others, my conscience was no less troubled by frequently selfish thoughts, words and deeds.

What I needed was some forgiveness. Forgiveness from those that I had wronged. But also a forgiveness that came from elsewhere for all those things of which I was ashamed and which no one else knew about. Sometimes thoughts and feelings are directed against others who are completely unaware of what you are feeling and thinking. To ask their forgiveness would require you to tell them what exactly you thought about them. That would make the offence worse. But even when you receive the forgiveness of another person the conscience may still be troubled. Indeed the more freely another forgives you the greater may be your distress.

It was to this human need for forgiveness that I found the appeal of Jesus to be most strong. Jesus had come into the world with the offer of God's forgiveness. The woman caught in the act of adultery he forgives. The man sick from a troubled conscience to the point of physical paralysis receives from Jesus the forgiveness of God. The men with murderous thoughts who nail Jesus to the cross hear from his lips a prayer that God might forgive them. Forgiveness and a peaceful conscience is the healing that comes from God through Jesus. It is not surprising that it should be called Good News.

This offer of forgiveness by Jesus was considered outrageous by his contemporaries, especially by the community's religious leaders. When Jesus forgave the paralysed man, several of the leaders questioned his right to do so. Who did he think he was? And when you think about it you can understand why they objected. Imagine encountering two strangers and seeing one of them hit the other; if you went up to the assailant and assured him that you were now going to forgive him he would be, to say the least, bemused. What right had you got to forgive him? You did not know him and after all it was not you that he was harming. So when Jesus is confronted with a stranger who has never done him any harm and assures him of forgiveness, those looking on are equally surprised. 'How can you say this? Only God can forgive sins.'

Reading between the lines of the account in Mark's gospel, you feel the author saying, 'Point made.' Jesus had a unique relationship with God. Like a Son. The forgiveness that belongs to God alone is for Jesus to give. It is to Jesus that we are to look for the forgiveness that alone can bring peace to the troubled conscience.

Now it is a difficult exercise to examine your conscience. Too much introspection can be a dangerous thing. Furthermore there are some of us who have such a low opinion of ourselves that we are only too ready to hate ourselves and then comfort ourselves in self-pity. And yet in the search for God it is right to let his light shine on our lives. Try to recollect those things which stir in you a sense of shame and are on your conscience. The God of love is a God of forgiveness. Jesus promises us that God will forgive us.

'God, my conscience is troubled by things of which I am ashamed. I know that I need forgiveness – the forgiveness of others and your forgiveness.'

25

Jesus said to her: 'Your sins are forgiven . . . go in peace.' (Luke 7:48,50)

8

Peace

A few years ago a very successful publisher was being interviewed on BBC radio. He was asked if he could sign up anyone in the world to write a book, who would it be and what would be the subject. The publisher seemed to have no doubts: 'Pope John Paul II on "Peace of Mind".' The interviewer seemed rather surprised by this choice and suggested (it appeared to me rather dismissively) that the book would sell some thousands of copies. The publisher, who had made his fortune by knowing his market, was quick to point out that the sales would be in their millions. I do not know the religious disposition of this man but I trust his assessment – that in our society today one of our greatest needs is to find peace. Not simply peace which is the absence of strife between nations and between conflicting factions in society, although God knows we need this too. It is the peace *within* that we need. It is that peace which almost defies description and passes understanding. It is a peace that is noticeable by its absence. It is a peace recognisable by its presence. This peace does not mean freedom from the inner restless quest for adventure nor does it mean the quenching of the fire of human passion. Nor does it mean the denial of the energetic instinct to express ourselves and communicate. Nor does it mean being set free from that inner turmoil that is so often exciting and creative. The peace that we seek is not the removal of these God-given energies. Such a peace would be not only vacuous but de-humanising. The peace that we thirst for is that in all these things we should experience wholeness. Yet this wholeness is often under threat.

There are all sorts of reasons why peace within is not our experience. It can be squeezed out by anxiety or by guilt or by fear or by hatred. These are just some of the cuckoos in the nest. These feelings are so real and take such a hold on the soul, the core of our being, that we have no power to shake them off.

Anxiety can be crippling. We try not to be anxious, but inside we feel torn apart. The emotions struggle with the will. We long for peace, but anxiety overwhelms us.

Guilt destroys our inner peace. There are feelings of guilt that arise from a conscience troubled by some past event or by some present situation for which we are responsible. The secret is hidden from the world, but not from our self. The heart longs to laugh again but the laughter sounds hollow, for there is no joy or peace within.

Fear can take such a tight grip of our mind and heart that peace vanishes to the point of no return. Perhaps it is a fear of the future or the fear of some other person, or even the fear of what you yourself might become.

Hatred too is the destroyer of inner peace. A heart consumed with hatred and the destruction of others is void of serenity. There is no peace here, only

28

violent turmoil. The object of our hatred may even be ourself. The person who was never loved and always felt rejected eventually learns to treat himself as he has been treated. He has felt despised, so he comes to despise himself. He cannot accept himself. He cannot forgive himself. He cannot love himself. He hates himself. He is restless and seldom at peace.

Sometimes none of these conditions of peacelessness may be our fault. We may have become victims of circumstance and the will and whims of others. We are casualties in a peaceless world. But even if these conditions are not our fault they are our responsibility. It is up to us how we respond and what we do in and to the conditions in which we find ourselves. We are responsible to ourselves if nobody else. We cannot blame anyone else if we do not try to do something about those things which rob us of peace.

It is to the experience of peacelessness that Jesus speaks. 'Peace I leave with you; my peace I give to you; not as the world gives do I give to you. Let not your hearts be troubled, neither let them be afraid' (John 14:27).

This peace has to be worked out differently in the lives of each one of us according to our situation and needs.

If guilt denies us peace then we may find the peace of God in the forgiveness of Jesus.

If self-hatred denies us peace then we may find the peace of God through the way Jesus loves and accepts the most disreputable, including ourselves.

If fear denies us peace then we may find the peace of God in the way that Jesus shows us the divine purpose being worked out in every and even difficult situations.

If anxiety denies us peace then we may find the peace of God through the healing presence of the risen Jesus.

Obviously these experiences of the peace of God will vary from person to person. We have been shaped and created differently but nevertheless we share the same instincts. The quest for peace may not be so obvious as the drives for self-preservation and the appetite for food, drink and sexual fulfilment, but it is there in every single human being.

So when God who made us comes to us with a message of peace there are many ready to listen. Since God created us with this desire for inner peace it is to God that we look to satisfy this need.

Consider all the pressures, both internal and external, that rob you of inner peace.

Meditate on the word 'peace'. Turn this word over in your mind. Slowly. Repeating it at intervals.

As you breathe out, imagine you are expelling all the hindrances to peace.

As you breathe in imagine you are receiving the peace of God.

Jesus said: 'My own peace I give you, a peace the world cannot give, this is my gift to you.' (John 14:27)

9

Love

We were in the middle of a heated discussion about
the state of the world and arguing about different
political solutions. Someone, under the influence of
a song of the day, tried to trump the debate by
insisting, 'All we need is love. What the world needs
is love. All we've got to do is just love each other.'
The man's enthusiasm, which had taken hold of him
and grew with every word, was punctured when
someone interrupted, '*Just* love each other? Have
you ever tried it?' The cynical realism of this bucket
of cold water pointed up an important truth about
the state of the world. Love may well be the solution.
But how do you do it?

Love is a difficult word. Not only because it is
hard to do, but also because it is not easy to pin down
what it means. When I say, 'I love black pudding', it
has an altogether different meaning from 'I love my
wife'. And even when we limit the word 'love' to
relationships between people we still use it in a
variety of ways. 'I love my grandmother' has a
completely different feel from 'I love beautiful
blondes'.

'Love' covers a range of different relationships. It
can mean passion, the physical and sexual desire for
another person. It can mean affection, for example,

the devotion a parent might feel towards his children. It can mean a deep friendship that might well exist between two people of the same sex. These different expressions of love do, however, have one thing in common. In order for them to survive, they need to be returned and reciprocated.

When you meet somebody you like you begin to open up to him in the hope that he too will begin to share something of himself with you. But if this person does not want anything to do with you friendship becomes impossible. Every attempt you make to become his friend is rebuffed. It is a painful and sometimes humiliating experience to have your offer of friendship rejected. And although you may try for some time, in the end your feelings of friendship evaporate and may even give way to indignation and resentment.

The same thing occurs when you fall passionately in love with someone. You are overwhelmed with a passion for this person and crave for the moment when you can touch him or her and be physically and sexually together. You long for that moment of ecstasy and abandonment when the two of you become one. But if the person for whom you have this passion ignores you, what then? If he denies you and rejects your overtures, what will happen to this passion? You may continue to love him for years but in the end the passionate feelings give way to disappointment and frustration. Unrequited passion eventually dies and may even be replaced by jealousy and hatred.

Affection, which describes the feelings that members of a family have for each other, is often more deeply rooted for it is in these relationships that we find our initial security. But even this love has its limits. The love of a parent can be stretched and tested. But if a child, especially when he has become an adult, continually scorns and despises the affections of his parents, then their hearts may well break and their love turn to bitterness.

So friendship, passion and affection can survive only when the object of their attentions returns their love. Human love has its limits. But although this is the love that makes the world go round, this is not the love that is likely to solve the problems of the world. For the problems begin when the love ends. What the world needs is a different sort of love. A love that knows no limits. A love that will not end. A love that will continue even when the person being loved scorns and rejects the lover. What the world needs is a love that loves people when they do not deserve to be loved. A love that will insist on forgiving those that hurt him. A love that will love even his enemies. There is no word in the English language to distinguish this sort of love. Perhaps we should call it supernatural love. It is the love that continues to love regardless of whether it is returned. It is the love that continues to burn even when its fires are not stoked by the fuel of appreciation. This love is different from and above our natural human loves.

It is this love which marked out Jesus. He taught people to love like this. And when they drove nails through his hands, not even then did he withdraw his love from his enemies. He loved them to the end. And this is the love with which God loves us.

Even though we may spend most of our lives ignoring God, he loves us. Were God's love a merely human love, he would have given us up years ago. No human being would stand the sort of treatment mankind has meted out to God down the ages. But God's love is greater. He loves us with all his heart. It is an act of his will that he chooses to love us. He loves us with all his strength. All the energy of God is channelled into caring for his creation. For you and me.

In discovering this love for ourselves we might well ask, 'But why does he love me?' The only answer that comes to us is simply, 'Because he loves me.' If God loved us for some reason or for some ulterior motive then it would not be love. You can see this even in a human relationship. If you loved a woman because she was fabulously wealthy and for what you could get out of her then the feelings you had for her would not be love. Genuine love means you love a person simply because you love her. That is why love is a mystery. There is no rhyme nor reason to it. And God's love for us is a mystery. He loves us because he loves us. He loves you because he loves you. He loves me because he loves me. Why? Because he loves me.

This love that loves a person, no matter who he is or what he has done, is supernatural. It is divine love. This is the love that the world needs. It is the love that we need.

Come down, O Love Divine,
Seek thou this soul of mine.

Try to memorise these words. Close your eyes and repeat them slowly.

Jesus said: 'You must love the Lord your God . . . You must love your neighbour as yourself.' (Mark 12:30–1)

10

Suffering

My first experience of tragedy was when my cousin was killed in a road accident. Kenneth was the eldest son and his mother was my mother's only sister. I shall never forget the moment when these two sisters met before the funeral. The embrace. The tears. The aching sobbing. The twinning of two souls in grief. I cried inside. 'Why, God? Why?' How could God allow such a thing to happen? My aunt asked me to stand with her and to say a prayer by Kenneth's grave. I do not know how I found the words or the voice to speak aloud, but I closed my eyes and prayed. My aunt fell to her knees and then prostrate before the grave. 'Lord, you know the pain of a mother losing her son . . .' The words were inadequate, but I remember they seemed to be accompanied by a serenity that came to my aunt and to all those who stood around the grave. For me it was with that desperate prayer that I began to make a discovery about God.

It was a discovery that led to the answering of a different question. Not 'Why did God allow it?' but 'Where was God in all this suffering and pain?'

Calling to mind the tragedy of Jesus on the cross I began to see the glimmer of an answer. God is here at the graveside. He is with us. In Jesus he knows what it is like to be tragically bereaved. He knows what it is like to leave and lose someone you love. God knows the heartache, the grief, the sense of loss. In Jesus God has felt all the pain of this moment. He knows. As a son dying before his mother's eyes Jesus, the son of Mary, felt her grief and her sorrow. As a son dying in the sight of God his Father Jesus, the Son of God, felt all the loss and loneliness of dying.

But what good is that? What consolation does that bring? What shred of difference does it make? I was once trying to comfort a grief-stricken person who turned on me with understandable bitterness. 'You don't know what it's like.' The comfort of someone who has gone through the same experience is always more real and consoling. Those of us caught up in the breakdown of a marriage or the death of someone close or some other human tragedy find greater help from those who have gone through the same things. Jesus becomes important to those of us who suffer because in him we can see that God knows what it is like to go through the hell of what we are going through. In Jesus God is with us. God knows what it is like to cry in agony; God knows what it is like to die in pain; God knows what it is like to be deserted by your friends; God knows what it is like to feel rejected and hated. These are but a few of the human experiences in which Jesus shared.

In our suffering we often feel alone and abandoned. We feel isolated from other people and forsaken by God. When we see Jesus more clearly, we realise that God is not as far off as we think. God is not a spectator of our pain. He cares for us not at a distance. He loves us by coming to our side.

He shows us the wounds of Jesus. He comforts us with the words, 'I know what it's like'.

In your own search for God there may well be the obstacle of suffering. You may have suffered some personal tragedy and even at this moment be going through some painful experience. You will have frequently asked God, 'Why?'
As you recall the pain and hurt before God, pray:

'God, where were you? God, where are you?'

Then try to picture Jesus dying on the cross.

Jesus said: 'The Son of Man was destined to suffer grievously, to be rejected' (Mark 8:31)

11

Death

I was once asked to take part in a BBC religious broadcast. The service was to take place in a crematorium chapel. The only problem with this was that there was not a regular congregation. It had to be bussed in. And it was decided to invite the relatives of all those who had been cremated in the previous year. The chapel was packed. I had a small part to play in the proceedings and was ushered to my place in front of a microphone. There on the seat was a white card with my name embossed in black letters. Flattered, I picked it up, then on the reverse side read the words 'In Memoriam'. A chill went down my spine. This was my first experience of a crematorium and although I have been to several since I am no more reconciled to this way of bidding farewell to people than I was then. However well the service may be conducted, the whole atmosphere is clinical. The coffin disappears behind some moving curtain or into a mechanical vault. People hardly realise the coffin has gone. It all seems to underline our well-known difficulty in coming to terms with death in this day and age. Not all cultures seem to have such problems. Although the Indian way of cremating their statesmen in public might at first strike us as morbid, there is something open and healthy about paying our respects in this way. Here is the body, now an empty shell, like a suit of old clothes, loved and well-worn, being set aside. There is dignity. There are memories. But the person is no longer there. The body reminds us of him. But the body is no longer him. The dust returns to dust, ashes to ashes.

Not long after this experience in the crematorium I went with a friend to visit an old lady who was dying. She had been the village schoolteacher for years and now in her nineties had an agile mind but an ageing body that had run its course. There was a radiancy about this lady who knew she had not long to live. She had been visited by many in the village, and gave former pupils of several generations mementoes from her possessions. I was received by this lady who seemed as if she were holding court. She was regal, not in the sense that she dominated but in the way that she drew the attention of all of us. Our eyes focused on this frail body and our hearts were captivated by her serenity. She viewed the prospect of her death with peace. My friend told me that she had even planned her own funeral service. It was not to be a morbid occasion but there were to be hymns of thankfulness and joy. Before we left the old lady prayed. Her voice, like her body, was frail but charged with emotion:

'The Lord is my shepherd; I shall not want . . .
He restoreth my soul . . .
Yea, though I walk through the valley of the shadow of death,
I will fear no evil: for thou art with me . . .
and I will dwell in the house of the Lord for ever.'

I have never heard these famous words said with such conviction. There was a beauty and a strength in her spirit. In her own words she talked about 'going home'. She even expressed the wish that she might die on Easter Sunday. She died two weeks later and 'went home'. Apparently the service in the local chapel lived up to her expectations – there was a note of triumph and a song of joy that were rooted in her conviction that death was not the end of the road.

Death of course is the great social leveller. No one will escape its power. However rich, influential or powerful, however poor, insignificant and powerless, we are all bound together in this common fate. And perhaps it is not until we have come to terms with dying that we have fully grasped the purpose of living. The clinical atmosphere of the crematorium chapel is a symptom that many of us are still bewildered, confused and distressed by the thought of death. But, as an old schoolmistress discovered, it need not be like that.

Listen again to these words: 'Though I walk through the valley of the shadow of death, I will fear no evil.'

Jesus said: 'If anyone believes in me, even though he dies he will live.' (John 11:25)

12

Life

My three-year-old daughter could hardly wait. We
had just bought a packet of sunflower seeds. We had
to plant them immediately. We filled a coffee jar
with some earth from the garden and carefully
buried the seeds beneath the surface. Then we
watered them – or, to be more accurate, flooded
them – and placed the jar on the window sill. Then
came the question, 'Where are the flowers, Daddy?'
I explained how we had to wait and how one day
we would see a little shoot peeping through the
surface. So every day we would take down the jar
to see if anything had happened. Since I have never
been a successful gardener I had planted more than
a few seeds, in the hope that at least one or two
might rise from the earth. The prospect of nothing
happening filled me with anxiety. My credibility as
a father was at stake. Fortunately in time every
single one of the seeds took root and shot through
the surface, much to the delight of my daughter.
There was a look of genuine wonderment in her eyes
when she first saw the shoots. I imagined that for
her what she was looking at was some sort of
miracle. Then came the next question. 'Where are
the seeds, Daddy?' 'Well, what you see there, those
are the seeds.' 'But, Daddy,' she persisted, as if I

had not understood the question, 'where are the *seeds*?', emphasising the last word with a long and impatient vowel.

'The seeds aren't there any more.'

'But where are they?'

'Well, they've become these little flowers.'

At that point my daughter lost interest and changed the subject.

It is difficult to explain to a three-year-old that a seed dies and its shell decays, but that in its dying gives birth to something else which is the same but totally different in its substance and appearance.

It must be as hard for the child's mind to understand this as it is for the adult mind to believe in his own life after death, and to grasp that a body dies and its shell decays but that in its dying gives birth to someone else who is the same but totally different in substance and appearance.

The advantage that we have over the child's mind is that we can observe this pattern of life out of death all around us. It is the story of nature.

The dying seed that rises from the earth to become a living flower provides us with a picture and a hope that death is not the end. God has made a world where autumn and winter give way to spring and summer. If the humble seed is given the hope of life after death, is it too fanciful to believe that people themselves also share in a similar hope?

There are many stories of people who have died momentarily and have been resuscitated and speak of an experience of life beyond death. The relevance of Jesus lies in the demonstration that here is a person who died like a seed yet who rose from the earth the same person but with a body different in substance and appearance. The story of the resurrection of Jesus is simply the human version of the story of the seed and the flower.

In your imagination place a seed before you. Or even take a real seed and focus your attention on it. Explore the process of planting and burying the seed; the growing of roots and the shoot; the flowering of the plant.

Meditate on these words: 'In dying there is life.'

Jesus said: 'It is written (in the scriptures) that the Christ would suffer and on the third day rise from the dead.' (Luke 24:46)

13

Jesus

I shall never forget the moment when I opened the Sunday newspaper and saw for the first time the Shroud of Turin. They say this is the shroud in which Jesus was wrapped when taken down from the cross and buried. And they claim that the face imprinted on the shroud is the face of Jesus. It is a haunting picture and the piercing gaze of those deep-set eyes disturbed me. Was this really Jesus? Is this what he looked like?

I imagined the face speaking; being angry; talking softly; challenging; comforting; and even crying. Was this the face of the man nailed to a cross? Was this really Jesus? Whether or not it was, and the experts are divided, the picture possessed a rare fascination for me and for any who wonder what Jesus looked like.

The only thing I found difficult to imagine this face doing was laughing. Yet judging from the stories he told Jesus was not without a sense of humour. He often told stories about larger-than-life characters in ridiculous situations. A clergyman trying to swallow a camel; a man with a great plank of wood shooting out of his eye, trying to remove a speck of dust from his friend's eye; a man who owed the equivalent of five times the country's total tax revenue. These humorous stories would surely have creased his face with laughter. And it is in Jesus' humour that his warmth as a human being comes through. But it is this very thing that often fails to come across when people either portray or try to imagine what he looked like. The problem is that none of the writers of the books in the New Testament tells us anything about his appearance. It is left to artists and film producers to give us their impressions. And often the films and paintings, the plays and statues, present him as an other-worldly being. Robert Powell, in Zeffirelli's *Jesus of Nazareth*, gives us a Jesus who glides from scene to scene with wide staring eyes, as if he has stepped straight out of an oil painting. Illustrations in children's Bibles reveal Jesus as a white Anglo-Saxon with well-groomed light brown hair, standing in a freshly laundered robe. The thought that he would have had dirt under his fingernails, needed a bath, opened his bowels and performed other bodily functions, is remote from the image that many have. And yet, by all accounts in the New Testament, he was a man of his time from the crown of his head to the tip of his toenails. He was often tired, needed to sleep, he ate and drank like any other person. And he sometimes cried. He was no superman. Beads of sweat were not foreign to his body. He was one of us 'from the womb to the tomb'.

And yet Jesus was different from us. The difference was not one of physical strength. It was a difference in moral courage. He possessed an inner strength that singled him out from his own contemporaries. He was a man of contrasts. He was compassionate with those who, whether rich or poor, were social outcasts, yet he vehemently opposed those who oppressed others. He was accepting of all men, women and children but outspoken against all expressions of evil. He loved everybody but hated everything that was destructive of God's creation. He was selfless but at the same time was aware of his own importance. He loved life yet was aware throughout that his destiny would involve him in a cruel and agonising death. And even as he died he loved and prayed for forgiveness for his assassins. It is little wonder that many people who would not call themselves Christians admire the man and hold him up as an example to the human race.

However it is in the comparing of ourselves with Jesus that we are made all the more aware of our lack of moral courage and our own inner contradictions. On the one hand we too have the same desire for truth that he had but on the other we find that deceit comes all too easily. We long for a world where love might rule but are taken aback by the quickness of our own reactions to hate those who hurt us. We are fascinated by the supernatural yet resist the belief in God. We are quick to judge but resent being judged by others. We try to lead good lives but never fully succeed. There is a gravity that pulls us down and prevents us from being the people we would like to be.

In some ways we can feel that all this distances us from Jesus. But, like a doctor whose mission in life is to heal the sick and not the healthy, Jesus comes to help those who cannot help themselves.

Assess your own strengths and weaknesses. What aspect of Jesus' character inspires you? In what way do you fall short of this? Ask God to help you to be more like Jesus.

Jesus said: 'It is not the healthy who need the doctor, but the sick. I did not come to call the virtuous, but sinners.' (Mark 2:17)

14

Image

In a dull moment when the children need to be entertained I sometimes take a piece of paper, lay it over a coin and gently rub the surface with a pencil. As I shade over the coin, so the image of the Queen's head comes through on to the paper. The image of the metal coin, now hidden and invisible, becomes apparent again on the paper in a different material.

In a similar way in the flesh and body of Jesus Christ the image of the invisible God comes through to us. God is hidden from our eyes. He is Spirit. We cannot see him. But in Jesus we see this image of God. In the material of human flesh the image of the invisible God becomes visible and apparent. In fact Jesus is the answer to all of us who have questioned, 'Well, if there is a God, why doesn't he show himself? Why doesn't he make himself known?'

Yet it is at this point that we feel the tension of a contradiction. On the one hand, as serious seekers after the truth, we call on God to play his part, declare his hand and reveal himself, and on the other hand we resist the idea that a human being could be the revelation and image of the God that we seek. We are sceptical about claims to being divine, not least because the human being in question lived such a long time ago. Perhaps we feel that the people he convinced that he was the image of God were uneducated peasants and easily persuaded. In fact the people of his day were remarkably well-educated in that every male Jew was taught through the local synagogue to read, write and question. Therefore the men who surrounded and followed Jesus were well able to scrutinise his integrity and keep written records of what he said and did. But more importantly, because the Jews took their religion so seriously and revered God so awesomely, they were resistant to the claims of any man who made himself out to be equal with God. If today somebody lays claim to being divine we treat him with mild amusement and recommend that he sees a psychiatrist. If you made such a claim in first-century Palestine, they would either stone you or throw you off a nearby cliff. Anyone who claimed to be uniquely at one with God, so that whoever saw him saw God himself, and anyone who usurped God's prerogative by offering forgiveness to sinners, and anyone who accepted the worship of men and women, was deemed guilty of blasphemy. The punishment was death. And this was the fate of Jesus, the image of God.

What is astonishing is that, in a culture that was even more resistant than our own to the idea that a human being could be God's unique revelation, this belief took root and flourished. The reason for this lay in the unassailable integrity of Jesus and in the surprise of his resurrection. Whatever else we may want to say about this latter event, it is clear from the New Testament that his rising from the grave was the strongest demonstration that Jesus was the

Son of God. Indeed if his body had rotted in the tomb his claims to being divine would have been seriously weakened.

If we ask ourselves what we would expect of someone who was God's image on earth, we discover through the gospels that Jesus matches these requirements. As you read the gospel, ask yourself and God, 'Is this the image of God?' Whenever you sense the answer 'Yes', then thank God for this revelation of himself.

Jesus said: 'To have seen me is to have seen the Father.' (John 14:9)

15

Crisis

In my early twenties I became a schoolteacher. Like most young teachers I felt very nervous, especially about being able to keep control in the classroom. I also wanted to be a popular teacher who got on well with the pupils and commanded their respect. I vividly remember arriving to take the first lesson of the fifth form class. I was welcomed at the door by a couple of heavies who informed me with a smile that they had given my predecessor a nervous breakdown. When I got to my desk there was a brick on it inscribed 'Mr Jones. Good luck. Luv. 5H1.'

I also clearly remember the day I meted out some punishment and was challenged by one of the culprits with, 'I shall hate you for the rest of my life!' The young man spat out his promise with such bitterness that it almost stunned me. I was always reluctant to punish people but if I had any aspirations to be a good teacher it seemed to me that I had to act against things that were wrong. I could hardly rate as a good or a caring teacher if in my classes I turned a blind eye to, say, bullying or cheating. A teacher who ignored the victimising of the smaller weaker members of the class could hardly be ranked as a loving teacher. Indeed a good teacher would be expected to act against and stop anything that was bad. Similarly a parent would have failed miserably if, in the name of love, he refused to take action against his older children terrorising the younger ones. 'How', we would ask, 'can a loving parent not do something about this?' What we are expecting the parent to do is to judge between the good things and the bad things and then to act against the bad things.

Just as we expect good human beings to act against evil, so too we expect God himself to do something about it. 'Why doesn't God do something about the state of the world? Why doesn't he put an end to all the evil?' When we see some of the terrifying brutality on the news, deep down we cry out for God to do something to end it all. When we feel this longing we are echoing a call for God to judge the world, to separate out the bad from the good, to act against the bad and, if possible, to wipe it out of existence. In effect, from our hearts we are asking this good God to be a judge. We are making a plea for divine judgment. And yet when we hear about the judgment of God many of us think, 'But how can a God of love judge?' But in truth the real question ought to be, 'How can a God of love not judge? How can a God of love not take action against that which is evil?'

The judgment of God is never spiteful or vindictive. The judgment of God is always loving. The fire of God's judgment comes from the same heart which burns with a love for his world. So why then does not the God of love do something now to rid the world of evil? Let him judge the world and wipe from the face of the earth all the causes of human distress and misery.

Before we press the question too earnestly we need first to pause and consider whom we have in mind. Do we mean that God should remove every single person who has contributed to the total sum of human sadness? Who do we imagine then would be left? For who has never been the cause of hurt, harm and distress to another human being? In this sense the whole human race must come under the judgment of God, for who has not added to the evil in the world? The question presents us all with a crisis. And crisis is the Bible's word for judgment.

Consider for a moment those things which you have said and done that have hurt and distressed other people.

Imagine the reaction of God who in his love longs to remove the causes of such sadness.

'Lord, have mercy on me.'

Jesus said this is the judgment: 'that though the light has come into the world men have shown they prefer darkness'. (John 3:19)

16

Reunion

A woman discovered that her husband had been
having an affair. In this instance and perhaps
unusually she was entirely blameless in the breakdown of the relationship. Although devastated by
the discovery she decided to confront her husband
but to assure him that she still loved him and forgave
him and wanted to forget the affair. The husband
reacted by denying that he needed her forgiveness
even though he admitted the affair. 'Keep your
charity,' he shouted. 'I don't need your forgiveness.'
In spite of the hurt and sense of betrayal the wife
continued to love her husband even after the
marriage had legally ended. To this day she still
loves the man. But even if the woman were to love
him perfectly for all eternity the relationship
between them could never be restored until the
husband did two things – recognise that he had
wronged her, and accept the forgiveness which she
offered. The fact that the relationship remains
broken is no reflection on the love of the wife. Her
love never falters. The continuing breakdown lies in
the man's refusal to admit his need of her forgiveness. And in this one-sided refusal lies the obstacle
to any reunion.

Of course when people no longer get on with each

other it is usually six of one and half a dozen of the other. As the maxim goes: it takes two to make a fight. But it is possible for a relationship to be wrecked by one person and for just one person to prevent a reunion. It is possible for one party to be innocent and for the guilty party to make reconciliation impossible. Now, just as the husband's rejection of the wife's forgiveness made a reunion between them impossible, so too our reluctance to accept the forgiveness of God makes a reunion between him and us equally impossible.

In the person of Jesus Christ dying on the cross God offers his forgiveness to the whole world. He loves all of us, even though through our selfishness we are often the cause of someone else's hurt and sadness.

He forgives the whole world but not everybody is forgiven.

In order for God's forgiveness to be effective in restoring friendship it has to be accepted as well as offered, otherwise the relationship is for ever broken.

The fact that some people are not forgiven is no reflection on the love of God. It is not lacking. He loves the world with all his mind, heart and strength. He forgives the whole world – past, present and future. But people in the world can know this forgiveness only when they receive it.

The reunion between God and people rests on a forgiveness both offered *and* received.

The hindrances that bedevil us and keep us from being reunited with each other are the same as the obstacles that keep us at a distance from God. Pride stops us admitting that we have done wrong and

56

from recognising the need for forgiveness. One of the most uncomfortable human experiences is to have someone point up your own weaknesses and errors. We resist it either by denying the accusations or by finding some excuse or by blaming someone else or by changing the subject. Very seldom do we ever welcome the truth about ourselves. Our nature is flawed with pride. It cuts us off from one another and alienates us from God.

Yet God is persistent in his longing for a reunion with us. He never ceases to come to us with his forgiveness. For that grand reunion between God and man to happen in our own lives we need to admit our need of his forgiveness and receive it. It means we have to abandon our pride and be prepared to humble ourselves. But it is worth doing, for so much is at stake. The relationship between God and us is unrestored until this happens. The moment we receive the pardon of God the reunion begins.

The prayer 'Lord, have mercy on me' is met with these words of Jesus: 'You are forgiven'. Receive his forgiveness and thank him for the reunion.

Jesus said: 'And eternal life is this: to know you, the only true God, and Jesus Christ whom you have sent.' (John 17:3)

17

Seeing

Ever since I was a child I have had a fear of being anaesthetised. So far I have undergone two anaesthetics, one in a dentist's chair and the other in hospital. On both occasions coming to after the surgery has been a strange experience. At first, as your eyes open, you are not quite sure where you are or what has happened to you. You cannot make sense of your surroundings. The faces looking down at you are larger than life, yet remote. The sounds and the sourroundings seem distant. As you come to, you begin to remember something of the events that led you here and you realise (thankfully) that the operation must now be over. Gradually the people and the clinical smells become more real. The bewilderment evaporates as you begin to make sense again of the world about you. Becoming aware of God is rather like coming out of an anaesthetic.

For many years most of us are unaware of God. Our minds and our souls are anaesthetised. We are oblivious to the unseen world of God and his angels. We are asleep and dead to the world of the spiritual, like the anaesthetised body is dead to the world of the operating theatre. In this state the sleeping person is unaware of the surgeon and his activity, unaware of the state and condition of his own body, and unaware of the healing process. As the patient comes to, he gradually and often painfully becomes aware of the reality that he has been dead too. So too as the spiritual anaesthetic loses its grip over our mind and soul we slowly but surely become aware of God. At first all the talk about God seems unreal and far-fetched. It is difficult to make much sense of it. Ideas about God are remote and distant from our own experience. Yet gradually for some unknown reason God becomes more real. You cannot necessarily put a time and a date to this realisation but as you look back you can see that God, who was once so unreal to you, has become much less so. You discover also that something has actually happened to you. You realise that you are not as antagonistic as you used to be. There are still lots of questions but they are not so hostile. You begin to see yourself in a new light. Far from being the one who sought to impress upon himself and others his own goodness, there is a willingness to realise that you are not the person that you should be. There is a new understanding about your true self and about your need of God's forgiveness. And there is a realisation that this healing process of forgiveness has already started to happen within you. These new insights dawn on us like men and women coming round from an anaesthetic.

This gradual spiritual awareness is a common experience. Although we ourselves have to be willing patients, the source of the spiritual awakening is in God himself. He alone has the power to rouse us from this deep sleep and to see the world as it really is. Jesus himself made this point. He suggested that, in order for us to see God at the centre of everything and as king over the universe, we needed the help of God's Spirit. It is the work of God's Spirit to open our eyes. It is his task to bring us round out of the anaesthetic. It is the Spirit of God who gives us the sight to believe that God is the creator of the world. When we come to this belief it is a sign that our minds have been touched by the Spirit.

Jesus went on to say that it is the Spirit who helps us to see and understand what is true. He helps us to face the truth about ourselves. Instead of allowing us to think that we are better than everyone else he makes us aware, often painfully, that we are a good deal worse. In particular the Spirit helps us to face up to the truth that we need the forgiveness of God. When we become conscious of this it is another sign that the Spirit of God is bringing us round from the anaesthetic. He helps us to feel our needs and our dependency as acutely as a patient in a hospital bed.

Jesus went even further and emphasised that the Spirit's work was to help people understand the importance of Jesus himself. Many people get to the stage of saying, 'Yes, I believe in God but I don't see why Jesus is so important. Why do you keep going on about Jesus?' It is as if they were only half-way out of the anaesthetic. It is the Spirit who helps us to see that in Jesus alone God has made provision for our forgiveness and reunion with him. When we begin to sense the importance of Jesus, this is a further sign that our mind and soul are benefiting from the help of the Spirit of God. When we realise that in Jesus we have both the doctor and the medicine, then we are seeing the world as God sees it. We are out of the anaesthetic. We are no longer dead to the real world. We are awake and alive to the truth.

Consider the progress you have made in your thinking about God, yourself and Jesus. And thank God for his help.

In a moment of silence, bare your soul and open your mind to God.

> *'Spirit of God,*
> *help me to see God as the king of creation;*
> *help me to see myself as I really am;*
> *help me to see the importance of Jesus;*
> *help me to be aware of the truth.*
> *Amen.'*

Jesus said: 'When the spirit of truth comes he will lead you to the complete truth.' (John 16:13)

18

Freedom

Here is a spiritual exercise.

Place your left hand in front of you, palm upwards. Imagine this represents you in your search for God. You try to come close to God, to be a better person; you try to pray, to be more loving. Yet none of this seems to have much effect.

Now with your right hand place a book or some object to cover your left hand. This is a picture of the gravity that constantly weighs you down and prevents that closeness with God for which you long. You simply cannot get close to God, however hard you try. Such is the sense of failure that you could be tempted to give up altogether this attempt to reach God. You feel unable to rid yourself of the gravity which pulls you down. It is as if there is some great barrier between you and God and you are helpless to move it.

Now place your right hand in front of you, palm upwards. This represents Jesus. God knows that we are powerless to help ourselves. He knows that we cannot free ourselves of the gravitational pull that stops us being the people we would rather be and soaring to the heights of a close relationship with God. So he sends Jesus to our aid.

Now move your right hand and with the palm

cover the book and your left hand. Jesus comes to be at one with us. The major difference is that he himself is free of that barrier which cuts us off from god. He is innocent of the sin that separates us from God.

Now turn your hands so that the right is beneath the left. When Jesus died on the cross he took to himself the sins of all the world. Like a magnesium sulphate paste that draws poison from a sore, so Jesus drew to himself the sins of the world. And in that moment on the cross he felt the painful hell of being cut off from God his Father. Our sin did to him what it does to us and separated him from his Father.

Now move your right hand away to the right carrying the book. In taking to himself the sins of the world, Jesus carries them away from us.

Now turn your left hand, palm upwards. The result is that we are now freed from the sins that kept us from God. The gravity that kept us apart has been removed. There is nothing to stop us soaring into this close relationship with God.

The moment that we accept Jesus as the one who carries away our sins is the moment when we meet with God in a new and closer relationship.

Look again at your left hand freed from the weight that covered it.

Go over again in your mind the way the hand was freed.

Meditate on your hand with these words: 'Through Jesus I am free.'

Then say this prayer:

'Through Jesus I am free.
Through Jesus I am forgiven.
Through Jesus there is nothing that separates me
   from God.
Through Jesus I am at one with God.
Through Jesus I am accepted by God.
Through Jesus I am forgiven.
Through Jesus I am free.
Amen.'

Jesus said: 'Everyone who commits sin is a slave . . .
if the Son makes you free you will be free indeed.'
(John 8:34, 36)

19

Gratitude

Trying to persuade someone to say thank you is a frustrating task. Perhaps as a parent you have made a considerable sacrifice in order to buy your child a present. You have saved for some time, you have bought the present and in a cloak and dagger operation smuggled it into the house and hidden it in some obscure corner. You can hardly wait for the day when you can give the present, and you imagine the look on your child's face when she sets eyes upon it. The moment eventually arrives when you offer the gift. You look expectantly at your daughter as she opens the paper. The present is revealed and the child raises her eyebrow, murmurs some sound and turns to the next parcel. This is too much for you to take. 'Well, don't you like it then?' 'Oh, yep, yep, it's okay.' You wait for a word of thanks but none comes. Unable to control the indignation, you demand through clenching jaw, 'Well, say thank you then.' 'Oh, thanks,' she mumbles rather grudgingly. The vote of thanks has a hollow ring to it.

When someone is forced to say 'thank you' the words mean very little. Words of gratitude mean something only when they come from a willing and genuinely grateful heart. When a person says 'thank you' it has to come of his own accord. It must be spontaneous. It cannot be forced. Otherwise it is not gratitude.

This may be why in all the teachings of Jesus on prayer he never openly demands that we should say 'thank you'. Even in the famous Lord's Prayer that he gave us to use there is no line expressing gratitude. It is as if Jesus is making the point that when we get to that stage of thanking God it has to come from us, from our own hearts, of our own accord, spontaneously.

Like a parent bearing gifts for his children God showers us with his goodness, similarly longing that we might respond with gratitude. Yet, unlike the impatient parent, God waits and keeps on waiting. He does not force us into a half-nelson and squeeze meaningless words of thankfulness out of us. Patiently he impresses his love upon us, waiting for us to respond.

One of the most significant steps along the path towards finding God that is either overlooked or underestimated is this sense of thankfulness to God.

In appreciating the beauty of creation we find ourselves on occasion thanking God for this enjoyment.

When we come through some personal difficulty we find ourselves thanking God for the way things have worked out.

When we feel secure and happy in a close and loving relationship we sometimes find ourselves thanking God for all that this means to us.

These thoughts of thankfulness are steps along the way. They are a recognition that we are not the ones who stand at the centre of the universe. They are an acknowledgement that there is a God in whom we move and have our being. They are an expression that it is from God that all these good gifts proceed. God who loves is the God who gives.

His ultimate gift is his son Jesus Christ. Yet even here with all the sacrifice that this grand gift involved God does not force us into being grateful.

In the arms of Jesus outstretched on the cross he comes to us with assurances of his love and forgiveness.

To the man or woman or child who welcomes this gift with gratitude belongs a measure of joy and peace the like of which no other gift can bring.

> *'Lord, I thank you for the beauty of your world.*
> *Lord, I thank you for the times of difficulty when you have helped me.*
> *Lord, I thank you for those who love me and for all that this means to me.*
> *Above all, Lord, I thank you for your love.*
> *I thank you for the gift of Jesus Christ.*
> *I thank you for all that he has begun to mean to me.*
> *Amen.'*

Jesus said: 'Yes, God loved the world so much that he gave his only Son, so that everyone who believes in him may not be lost but may have eternal life.' (John 3:16)

20

Prayer

A great-aunt who was widowed in her thirties and lived to her nineties told me how she was often alone but never lonely. It was the presence of 'the Almighty' that gave her companionship and strength. Aunt Mary was evidently a lady who had found God. One day when we were together in her cottage in Brecon she talked about her faith. 'Each Sunday a father would walk through the valley to chapel with his young daughter. Hand in hand and dressed in their Sunday best, they would talk together along the way. In the early autumn when the leaves had already begun to fall and the road was slippery, they came to a muddy patch. The little girl stopped, looked up at her father and said, "Daddy, I think you had better carry me now." The father, without thought for his suit, stooped and scooped his daughter into his arms and carried her. That', urged my aunt with all the wisdom of her own experience, 'is faith. It's simply saying, "Daddy, I think you'd better carry me now." ' The intimacy between a child and a devoted parent is the relationship into which God draws us.

Jesus told us that in our prayers we should come to God and talk to him like a father. And when we pray to God as Father we get the right balance of intimacy and respect.

And here is the prayer which Jesus taught us.

Our Father in heaven,
hallowed be your name.
Your kingdom come,
your will be done,
on earth as it is in heaven,
Give us today our daily bread;
and forgive us our sins
as we forgive those who sin against us.
Lead us not into temptation
but deliver us from evil.
For yours is the kingdom, the power and the glory
for ever and ever. Amen.

We don't have to use this prayer. God encourages us to talk with him simply as we would to a parent. But when we are lost for words this, the Lord's prayer, can help express our feelings.

'Our Father in heaven'. Imagine how, as a parent, you would react to your children coming to you for help. How would you respond to their hugging you?

'Hallowed be your name.' Consider the times when for you 'God' has been no more than a swear word.

'Your kingdom come.' Welcome God to yourself as your king. In your imagination give him the orb and sceptre of your life. Pause for a moment and think of all that you own. Hand it to God the king.

'Your will be done on earth as it is in heaven.' The Father's will is to reconcile a world that is divided. People are separated from him and alienated from each other. His will is to reunite men and women to

himself. And in this reunion to unite divided families, divided countries, divided races and a divided world.

'Give us today our daily bread.' The Father has given us his own son Jesus Christ. This is his ultimate gift. Is he therefore likely to withhold from us anything less, either material or spiritual?

'Forgive us our sins.' The promise of God is that he both forgives and forgets. When we come to God confessing, 'I've done that thing again!' such is the Father's forgiveness it is as if he says, 'What thing was that?' Whatever may be troubling your conscience, if it has been confessed it is now forgiven and forgotten.

'As we forgive those who sin against us.' Consider those who have done you wrong whom you have not yet forgiven. How do their offences compare with yours against God? React to their sins as God has reacted to yours.

'Lead us not into temptation but deliver us from evil.' Think of any destructive pressures of which you may be aware. Either on you personally or on your family or in the world. It is important to remember that the power of God is greater than the power of evil. The two forces are not evenly matched. God is able to deliver us from evil.

'Yours is the kingdom, the power and the glory.' Repeat this phrase slowly to yourself. Bow your head and offer these words to God. Kneel and repeating the words offer yourself to God.

Jesus said: 'Say this when you pray: Father . . . What father . . . would hand his son a stone when he asked for bread?' (Luke 11:2, 11)

21

Worship

The time I first set eyes on the Jungfrau and the
Eiger mountains was a rare moment. As the train
moved up through the Lauterbrunnen Valley I stood
at the window speechless. The enormousness, the
vast majesty of these mountains was overwhelming.
Then as we drew nearer to the foothills I began to
express my amazement. 'Just look at those mountains. Have you ever seen anything like it? Aren't
they fantastic?' These and other inadequate words
poured out, probably to the boredom and dismay of
the other travellers. In my mind I was not with these
passengers in the train, who were more than likely
wishing that I was not there in body either! I was
not actually talking to anyone in particular. I was
simply giving expression to what was going on inside
me as I gazed out on this marvellous aspect of
creation.

Of course these spectacular and inanimate mountains did not need my adulation and worship. They
had existed for thousands of years and would
continue for many more without any need of my
songs of praise. I was worshipping them, acknowledging their beauty and their worth, not because
they needed it, but because I had a need to do so.

This experience helped me to understand what it

71

is that we do when we worship God. I used to worry that there was something not altogether right about God looking for his creatures to worship him. Knowing how much men and women thrive on praise and adulation and how willing they are to believe it, even when it is blatantly untrue, I wondered whether God's desire for us to worship him reflected some inadequacy on his part. Was he himself on some ego trip?

I came to see that God sought our praise not for his sake but for ours. Just as when we come face to face with beautiful scenery we acknowledge its worth, or just as when we hear some sublime music we give expression to our appreciation, so when we meet with God there is an inner urge to acknowlege his worth and worship him. God does not need such worship. No more than the mountains do. We need it. To be true to ourselves we need to give vent to our appreciation. When we encounter the truth in all its glory and majesty we need to give expression to the discovery. We cannot keep quiet. We need to say something. It is part of being human. To worship is to be human. The discovery of truth, the finding of God, demands proclamation. And God desires our worship for the very reason that to get to the point of worshipping him means that we have at last found him. The fanfare belongs to the finding. This is why Jesus said that God actively searches for people to worship him. Not for his sake but for ours.

And this is the truth which we discover. It is from God that we came. It is to God that we all return. It is in God that we live and move and have our being. God knows that we need to know this truth. Without knowledge of this truth we are rootless. We are like adopted children who sense that they do not belong until they have discovered their roots. And when we discover the true source of our being and experience reunion with the one who made us there is an inner urge to say so. This is worship.

Spend some time looking up into the sky. Imagine how the world must look to God.

> 'When I look up into the sky
> and see the work of your hands,
> the moon and the stars
> which you have made,
> I say to myself,
> What is man that you should even think of him,
> what is man that you should ever care for him?
> You have made him little less than a god.
> You have laid creation at his feet
> and put all things into his hands
> O Lord God almighty,
> your ways are remarkable.
>
> Praise the Lord, O my soul.
> Let everything within me cry out in praise.
> Praise the Lord, O my soul.
> Forget not God's goodness.
> He forgives me all my sins.
> He renews me with peace.
> He saves my life from ruin.
> He warms me with his love.
> Praise the Lord, O my soul.'

(from Pss 8, 103)

Jesus said: 'true worshippers will worship the Father

73

in spirit and truth: that is the kind of worshipper the
Father wants'.

(John 4:23)

22

Destiny

The work of a potter at his wheel throwing clay and moulding it is always full of surprise. Within a few minutes he has transformed the raw material into a graceful shape. Then suddenly and to the bewilderment of those looking on he presses in his thumb and seems to ruin what he has just created. But as he continues to work the clay slowly and surely, in the hands of a craftsman there emerges a new and more beautiful creation.

You and I are clay in the hands of God. All the time, whether we are aware or not, he is moulding us and shaping us. Sometimes we will see and understand what is going on and approve what is happening to us. Other times we will be mystified for we can see neither rhyme nor reason to what we are going through; we may find some experiences painful and either doubt or resent the way God is treating us. But in all the changing situations of our life God is at work to remake us.

As God models the clay the pattern which he holds before us is the image of Jesus. He is the one true person on whom all others are to be modelled. He is flawless while we are flawed. The will of God is that we should become like Jesus. This is our destiny. To be men and women of love.

Love is always patient and kind;
it is never jealous;
love is never boastful on conceited;
it is never rude or selfish;
it does not take offence,
and is not resentful.
Love takes no pleasure in other people's sins
but delights in the truth.

(1 Cor. 13:4–6)

This is what Jesus is like. And this is what God calls us to be.

Our immediate reaction is that to be like this would lead others to take advantage of us. I wish I could say that such a fear was misplaced. It is not. For it is more than likely that in loving our neighbours as ourselves and loving even our enemies we will be taken advantage of. To be committed to love will make us very vulnerable. Others may well take our strength of determination to love them as a sign of weakness. And far from moving them to change their own attitude they will insist all the more on going their own way. This is what happened to Jesus. And he left his followers under no illusion that this is what would happen to them.

'If anyone is considering following me, let him lose sight of himself and take up a cross and follow' (Mark 8:34).

'Taking up a cross' spoke to Jesus' followers of rejection. Before being executed a criminal had to run the gauntlet of carrying his cross through a hostile and jeering crowd. There was no sympathy here. The man who carried a cross was a social outcast.

It may seem to us rather an exaggeration to describe following Jesus in these terms. But perhaps that is a reflection on how so very few of us live up to the call of God. To strive for justice, to do something about the poor, to imitate the moral courage and the spiritual qualities of Jesus Christ, invariably produces from the world around us a mixed reaction of admiration and antagonism.

Yet whenever we find the path of love painful and costly we can strengthen our will to keep on loving by knowing we are walking in the footsteps of Jesus.

When people take advantage of us we know that they took advantage of him. When people reject us we remember that they rejected him. To see this does not lessen the pain and the anguish, especially when those who use us are those whom we love most deeply. There will be times when we are sorely tempted to give up and to give as good as we get. We will feel like throwing in the towel and abandoning the fight to love the world. We may even wish that God would leave us alone and let us be.

It comes as a surprise to us that although we are often tempted like this and frequently lapse into states of selfishness it has become impossible to escape the call of God.

Along the way of finding God something has happened to us. While we have been pursuing God he himself has been searching for us. There has been a mutual pursuit. And in the reunion with God, in the coming-together, his Spirit has brought about a change in us. We can no longer live our lives totally oblivious to his presence. Our consciences are too sensitive to let us get away with unbridled selfishness. We may fail many times but the call of God has become irresistible. God has come to us. We have welcomed him. And we can never be the same again. He simply will not let us go.

Jesus said: 'If anyone wants to be a follower of mine, let him renounce himself and take up his cross and follow me . . . And know that I am with you always; yes, to the end of time.' (Mark 8:34 and Matt. 28:20)

23

Beginning

Recently I returned to the place where I had lived when I was seven. I was startled by the difference between what I had remembered in my imagination and what was really there. The long road to our home was in fact a short lane, the lane from our house to the cliffs was a narrow path, the cliffs were large rocks and the bay barely a paddling pool. And yet to me as a young boy the length of the lane and the path and the size of the rocks and the pool were indeed great. Climbing the rocks required much effort and walking the lane many footsteps. It is not surprising that I should remember these things as greater than they actually were. But of course I would be wrong to discourage any child now living there and playing around these rocks by saying that they were mere trifles.

As you look back through this book and perhaps through the last few months and years you may well sense that you have come a long way down the road of finding God. But in another sense and from another point of view the journey both for you and for me has only just begun. God is infinitely greater than any of us can imagine. It is impossible for the finite mind with all its limitatons to plumb the depths of the infinite and the eternal. God has given us a path to walk down, some rocks to clamber over and water to splash around in. But this is only a corner of God's creation. And yet in this corner he has come to us. And if it is not too trivial an idea, he has come to play with us and to weep with us, to laugh with us and to mourn with us, to dance with us and to be still with us.

I began this book by the sea. I wrote about wanting to reach out and hold creation to me – to be united with it and to be at one with creation. What I have come to see with the help of many friends, through several books including the Bible, through Jesus Christ and the help of God's Spirit, is that the Father of heaven and earth is moment by moment unfolding a plan not only to unite all creation but to reunite us all who live in this corner of the universe to the Creator himself.

And since some who have already read this short book have asked, 'Where do we go from here?' let me suggest some further steps.

Keep praying. Ask God to show you the way.

Keep searching. Find others who are on the journey and question them about their discovery.

Keep listening. Take time often to be quiet and to listen to God.

Keep reading. The Bible gives a unique record of the way God reveals himself. Avoid trying to read from Genesis to the end – you could easily get stuck in the books of Leviticus and Numbers. Concentrate on the gospels, the Psalms and the Letter to the Ephesians. And here are some other books which I have found helpful along the way:

Mere Christianity, *by C. S. Lewis, requires some effort but is excellent for showing how reasonable is the Christian faith.*

A Grief Observed, *and* The Problem of Pain, *also by C. S. Lewis, are helpful in coming to terms with the problem that the existence of suffering poses to those who believe in God.*

My God is Real, *by David Watson, is a straightforward and easily read book on what is involved in becoming a Christian.*

The Killing, *by Richard Holloway, is a short devotional book on the meaning of the death of Jesus Christ.*

Praying the Kingdom, *by Charles Elliott, is a challenging examination on what it means to pray the words, 'Your kingdom come'.*

Who moved the stone? *by Frank Morrison is an investigation by a sceptical lawyer into the evidence for the resurrection. His scepticism turned to belief under the weight of the evidence.*

And finally, as someone involved in the Church, I know only too well that it does not have the brightest image nor does it always appear very welcoming to the outsider. But I would encourage you to find a church locally and to persevere with it. Here you will find a community of fellow travellers. Some may well have tired of the journey but do not give them up. Your questions and experiences may even revitalise their flagging spirits.

In the Old Testament God said to a fellow traveller

by the name of Joshua: 'Have I not told you: Be strong and stand firm? Be fearless then, be confident, for go where you will, the Lord your God is with you.' (Joshua 1:9)

And this promise was echoed by Jesus to all his followers as he neared the end of his journey here on earth. 'And know that I am with you always; yes, to the end of time'. (Matt. 28:20)

24

Words of Jesus

Jesus said: 'Come to me, all you who labour and are overburdened, and I will give you rest . . . learn from me.' (Matt. 11:28)

Jesus said: 'I have come so that they may have life and have it to the full.' (John 10:10)

Jesus said: 'I have told you this so that my own joy may be in you and your joy be complete.' (John 15:11)

'Thomas said, " . . . how can we know the way?" Jesus said: "I am the Way".' (John 14:5–6)

Jesus said to her: 'Your sins are forgiven . . . go in peace.' (Luke 7:48, 50)

Jesus said: 'My own peace I give you, a peace the world cannot give, this is my gift to you.' (John 14:27)

Jesus said: 'You must love the Lord your God . . . You must love your neighbour as yourself.' (Mark 12:30–1)

Jesus said: 'The Son of Man was destined to suffer grievously, to be rejected.' (Mark 8:31)

Jesus said: 'If anyone believes in me, even though he dies he will live.' (John 11:25)

Jesus said: 'It is written (in the scriptures) that the Christ would suffer and on the third day rise from the dead.' (Luke 24:46)

Jesus said: 'It is not the healthy who need the doctor, but the sick. I did not come to call the virtuous, but sinners.' (Mark 2:17)

Jesus said: 'To have seen me is to have seen the Father.' (John 14:9)

Jesus said this is the judgment: 'that though the light has come into the world men have shown they prefer darkness'. (John 3:19)

Jesus said: 'And eternal life is this: to know you, the only true God, and Jesus Christ whom you have sent.' (John 17:3)

Jesus said: 'When the spirit of truth comes he will lead you to the complete truth.' (John 16:13)

Jesus said: 'Everyone who commits sin is a slave . . . if the Son makes you feel, you will be free indeed.' (John 8:34, 36)

Jesus said: 'Yes, God loved the world so much that he gave his only Son, so that everyone who believes in him may not be lost but may have eternal life. (John 3:16)

Jesus said: 'Say this when you pray: Father . . . What father . . . would hand his son a stone when when he asked for bread?' (Luke 11:2, 11)

Jesus said: 'true worshippers will worship the Father

in spirit and truth: that is the kind of worshipper the Father wants'. (John 4:23)

Jesus said: 'If anyone wants to be a follower of mine, let him renounce himself and take up his cross and follow me.' (Mark 8:34)

Jesus said: 'And know that I am with you always; yes, to the end of time.' (Matt. 28:20)